The
HOPE
H A N D B O O K
FOR COUPLES

POWERFUL, INSPIRATIONAL, HOPEFUL
TWEETS THAT ENCOURAGE MOTIVATE,
AND SPEAK TO YOUR SPIRIT

THE SEARCH FOR PERSONAL GROWTH

GERMANY KENT

STARSTONE

The Hope Handbook for Couples

Copyright @2015 by Germany Kent

Visit us online at www.TheHopeHandbook.com

ISBN: 978-1-943206-09-4 (ebook)
ISBN: 978-1-943206-10-0

Library of Congress Control Number: 2015904485

Compiled by Germany Kent

Published by: Star Stone Press, 10736 Jefferson Blvd #164, Culver City, CA 90230

Printed in the United States of America

Amongst inspirational tweets of hope compiled using wise words from my grandmother, original content, and tweets of knowledge from other tweeters, you will find words of hope passed along from many other wise people who have crossed my path on my journey to self-discovery. You will also find motivational messages as spoken or written by world leaders and motivational gurus.

Books are available in quantity for promotional or premium use. Requests for information should be addressed to: Star Stone Press, 10736 Jefferson Blvd #164, Culver City, CA 90230, for information and discounts and terms. You may also send a request at www.GermanyKent.com

CONTENTS

REFLECTIONS
MEDITATIONS
INSPIRATIONS

"Love is patient, love is kind. It does not envy, it does not boast, it is not proud. It is not rude, it is not self-seeking, it is not easily angered, it keeps no record of wrongs. Love does not delight in evil but rejoices with the truth. It always protects, always trusts, always hopes, always perseveres."

- 1 Corinthians 13:5-7

INTRODUCTION

Many believe love is easy and is a sensation that magically appears when "the perfect person" comes along. Truth is, love is very complex; it can be inspirational, magical, imaginary, joyous, or painful and pure madness all in one. Sometimes love can feel like Disney magic and other times like a battlefield.

Everybody wants to be in a relationship, but no one wants to give up being single. It happens more often than we think. Because deep, intimate love emanates present behavior, it is vital to display love and affection each opportunity that you have. To make a partnership successful, each person should allow for the individuality of each partner within the relationship. Following this practice helps to give each person their personal space, and freedom to be themselves. This also allows each person in the relationship to experience both oneness with and separateness from their partner.

The goal is for both people to experience a balance that is a complimentary sharing of love between both individuals in the relationship. Good relationships don't just happen. They take time, patience, giving and two people who truly want to be together. Quite often it is the compatible energy that keeps the relationship flowing. A relationship thrives when we are engaged in giving our all to the committed relationship; we begin to experience more fulfillment and joy.

Love can be made brand new, that is when we begin to experience the racing heart, butterflies, and urges to be together all the time, followed by a mutual liking of each other, this then leads to a deep friendship and a more intimate love connection.

The intensity many couples feel is usually great affection boosted by similarities in personality, life goals, sexuality, and hopes for the relationship.

A healthy relationship is always growing, and partners recognize change as valuable. Change allows the two of you to explore each other outside of your comfort zones, often leading to happier, more engaging and becoming more and more connected to each other with deeper levels of respect.

The best feeling in the world is to be in a relationship with someone who loves you for who you are. Seek to find a mate who will know your flaws, weaknesses and mistakes and still thinks you are still the best thing that has ever happened to them.

Practice recurring moments with your partner making an intentional effort to offer unconditional displays of love. Show rather than tell by practicing not only saying, "I love you," but showing it. While each of us is responsible for our own happiness, having a mate who compliments our own lifestyle; one who encourages, motivates, nourishes, inspires, and offers support,can make all of life's endeavors worthwhile.

Love people for who they are, and not for who you want them to be. Love is active and you must be grateful for small things, big things, and everything in between. Count your blessings, not your problems. No relationship is perfect, but with hard work, time and patience, it can be perfect for the two of you. If there has been hurt and disappointment in your relationship, but you are focused on moving forward, heal and move on. Wipe the slate clean and press on to new adventures and new love fests. There's no reason to look back when you have so much to look forward to. Here's to loving yourself and the power of love for others!

🐦 🐦 🐦

PART ONE

LOVE BEGETS LOVE

"Keep love in your heart. A life without it is like a sunless garden when the flowers are dead."

– Oscar Wilde

🐦 Love is perfect; we do not need to be.

🐦 You must first learn to love yourself before you can give love.

🐦 Each relationship is an opportunity to open your heart and connect with the soul of another person.

🐦 True love does not pay attention to the evil it suffers; it rejoices in being good.

Love is seeing an imperfect person perfectly.

Love is experiencing openness to change and explore the relationship.

🕊 True love has a foundation of integrity, respect, faith and trust.

🕊 Sometimes you need to distance yourself to see things clearly.

🐦 Sometimes your heart needs more time to accept what your mind already knows.

🐦 Love with every ounce of your bones.

🕊 Love must be experienced; it's meaning is infinite and can never be totally defined.

🕊 It's sad when people let past relationships ruin their future happiness.

🐦 Never jeopardize a good thing for a new thing.

🐦 The quality of what you actually embody is what determines whom you attract in your life. Like attracts like.

🐦 True love is the nature of bliss.

🐦 The beautiful thing about a hug is that as you're giving one, you're also getting one.

🐦 Love is like a virus, it can happen to anybody at any time.

🐦 Never expect, never assume, never ask, and never demand. Just let it be. If it is meant to be, it will happen.

🐦 Love is the most beautiful thing to have, hardest thing to earn and most hurtful thing to lose.

🐦 Be honest with people that love you: they deserve your honesty.

🕊 Love has no meaning other than the meaning "we" give it.

🕊 Find someone who wants you as much as you want them.

🕊 A true relationship is having someone who accepts your past, supports your present, loves you and encourages your future.

🕊 No matter how much you care about someone, sometimes it's not meant to be.

🐦 Second chances aren't always an option, so realize what you have.

🐦 If you get a second chance, don't mess it up.

🐦 Love is a bridge between two hearts.

🐦 Love is bringing out the best qualities in your partner.

🐦 A relationship is more than finding the
right person, it's also about being the
right person.

🐦 You only attract a more loving person by
becoming more loving yourself.

🐦 Love your mate for who he or she is, not for who you want them to be.

🐦 Love is giving someone the power to destroy you, but trusting them not to.

🐦 Be happy with yourself before you try to make someone else happy.

🐦 What comes easy won't last and what lasts, won't come easy.

🕊 Love is: loving someone without expecting anything in return.

🕊 You can't blame someone for walking away if you didn't do anything to make that person stay.

🐦 You will recognize true love by the way you are treated.

🐦 When someone shows you his or her true colors, don't try to paint a different picture.

🐦 Don't raise your voice; improve your argument.

🐦 One of the best feelings is laughing with someone and realizing halfway through how much you enjoy them and their existence.

🐦 A real relationship will make it through anything.

🐦 Love is the force that brings about unity and harmony.

🐦 Fall in love with someone's eyes and intelligence. They are the two things that never change.

🐦 If two people truly want to be together, they will find a way to make it work.

🐦 The best feeling of happiness is when you are happy because you've made somebody else happy.

🐦 Love, respect, and trust your mate.

🕊 Be with someone who brings out the best in you, not the stress in you.

🕊 There's a difference between what your mate wants and what your mate needs.

🐦 True love seeks the happiness and well being of your partner.

🐦 When you are not sure which way to go, it is always wise to follow your heart.

🕊 Loving someone should not mean losing yourself.

🕊 A good relationship is with someone who knows all your insecurities and imperfections but still loves you for who you are.

🐦 Your soul mate is someone who knows all about you and still loves you.

🐦 If you want to be trusted, then you have to be honest.

🐦 Life is a flower for which love is the honey.

🐦 Remember: The tighter the hug the better.

🕊 You have to love yourself because no
amount of love from others is sufficient
to fill the yearning that your soul
requires from you.

🕊 Live from this fresh moment and not
from what is old and dead.

When you finally get something good, enjoy it. Don't go looking for something better.

There is never a time or place for true love. It happens accidentally ins a heartbeat, in a single flashing throbbing moment.

🐦 You have to believe in love to be in love.

🐦 Be with someone who is proud to have you.

🐦 Love sometimes needs to take its course.

🐦 Love is when your partner knows you are not perfect, but treats you as if you are.

🐦 True love stands by each other side on good days and stands even closer on bad days.

🐦 Maybe it's not always about trying to fix something that is broken. Maybe it's about starting over and creating something better.

🐦 Make your mate smile even when you're not around.

🐦 The best things in life are not things; it's the people who make you feel loved and cared for.

🐦 If you love someone, showing them is better than telling them.

🐦 When you really care about someone, his or her happiness matters more than yours.

🐦 The best place in the world is in the arms of the one you love.

🐦 Some people cross your path and change your whole direction.

🕊 Be with people, who know your worth;
   you don't need too many people to
   be happy; just a few real ones who
   appreciate you for who you are.

🕊 Take care of the people you love, but
   take even better care of the people that
   love you.

🐦 Let someone love you just the way you are - as flawed as you might be.

🐦 The road to self-discovery is paved with Love.

PART TWO

COMMUNICATION RULES

"The most important thing in life is to learn
how to give out love, and to let it come in."
– Morrie Schwartz

🐦 "We are most alive when we're in love."

- John Updike

🐦 The first duty of love is to listen.

🐦 10% of conflicts are due to difference in opinion and 90% are due to wrong tone of voice. Remember this when trying to prove your point.

🐦 When she talks, just listen.

🐦 Always be thoughtful.

🐦 Talk is cheap.

🐦 If you don't mean it, don't say it.

🐦 Never let an opportunity pass by to tell someone that you love them; you care about them and they are important to you.

🐦 We all need someone to talk to, someone who listens, and someone who understands.

🐦 Always meet each other with a smile for the smile is the beginning of love.

🐦 When he talks, don't interrupt.

🐦 Never push a loyal person to the point where they no longer care.

🐦 Trust your intuition. You don't need to explain or justify your feelings to anyone.

🐦 Effective communication is a two-way process.

🕊 Choose your words carefully. Once they are spoken, they can only be forgiven, never forgotten.

🕊 Always let grace have the last word. We'll only lose the arguments our pride insists on winning.

🐦 Look through your heart and your
thoughts will reflect love.

🐦 No one really falls in love; love falls
in them. What happens next makes
a beautiful life. We're rivers, not
reservoirs.

🕊 Don't try to give advice when not asked.

🕊 Listen without defending and speak without offending.

🐦 Worrying is a waste of time; it doesn't change anything, it just messes with your mind and steals your happiness.

🐦 Don't play the role of therapist in your relationship.

🐦 People may not always tell you how they feel about you, but they will always show you. Pay attention.

🐦 Your heart knows things that your mind can't explain.

🐦 Over thinking does kill your happiness.

🐦 Your partner needs your smile, your laugh, your warmth and your existence.

🕊 Think positive, and positive things will happen.

🕊 Confidence is the ability to feel beautiful without needing someone to tell you.

🐦 If you make a mistake, apologize, not because of what it will get you, but because it's the right thing to do.

🐦 Your beliefs don't make you better, your behavior does.

🐦 You learn best by listening, observing, and truly hearing the other person.

🐦 The thing people want most from you is your focus and attention.

🐦 Conscious listening always creates understanding.

🐦 The most important thing in communication is hearing what isn't said.

🐦 When the trust account is high, communication is easy, instant, and effective.

🐦 Admitting when you are wrong is the greatest moral, intellectual, and creative leap you can make.

🐦 Your mind can change our behavior, and your behavior can change your outcome.

🐦 Do all things with kindness.

🐦 Physical attractions are common. A mental connection is rare.

🐦 Great conversation is more than just a verbal experience. It's the natural high for the conscious mind.

🐦 A lack of communication turns the smallest of issues into huge problems.

🐦 Why stress over something you can't change.

🕊 To admit you were wrong is to declare
you are wiser now than you were before.

🕊 Learn to listen a little more and shout a
little less.

🐦 Apologize for what you have done, but never apologize for who you are.

🐦 Do not listen with the intent to reply, but with the intent to understand.

🐦 True wisdom knows when to speak and when to remain silent.

🐦 Never ignore a person who loves you, and cares for you.

🐦 Love should grow. Mistakes are opportunities to grow.

🐦 Love is just a word but you bring it definition.

🐦 It is never too late to make things right.

🐦 Don't ruin a great moment to prove a good point.

🐦 If it is important to you, you will find a way. If it's not, you'll find an excuse.

🐦 Cultivate love and you will find a deep trust in life emerge from within you.

🕊 You can have friendship and you can have love, but it's only when you have both together that it will be a great love.

🕊 In conflict stay calm. Lose your mind and you lose the battle.

🐦 Radiate Love.

🐦 Be with someone who can make you laugh when you don't even feel like smiling.

🐦 Drama in speech leads to drama in relationships. Tame your tongue.

🐦 Too often the tongue cannot convey what the heart feels.

🐦 Say it, before it's too late.

🐦 Raise your words, not your voice. It is rain that grows flowers, not thunder.

🐦 A good mate accepts who you are, but also helps you become who you should be.

🐦 Everyone makes mistakes. If you can't forgive others, don't expect others to forgive you.

🐦 Make sure your mate knows how important they are in your life before it's too late.

🐦 There's a difference between hearing somebody and listening to them.

🐦 You don't really understand a woman until you know every word she's not saying to you.

🐦 Love is patient, kind, gentle, long-suffering and keeps no record of wrongs. It believes, hopes and endures all things. Love never fails.

🐦 The first to apologize is the bravest. The first to forgive is the strongest. The first to forget is the happiest.

🐦 A soul mate is someone who knows all about you and still loves you.

🐦 A good woman doesn't leave based on opportunity, but a wise woman never stays in a relationship where she isn't valued.

🐦 Ladies that carry themselves as queens inspire men to behave like kings.

Men who carry themselves as kings
inspire women to behave like queens.
Royalty attracts royalty.

PART THREE

LOYALTY MEANS EVERYTHING

"Love is when the other person's happiness is
more important than your own."

– H. Jackson Brown, Jr.

🐦 Infatuation is when you find somebody who is absolutely perfect. Love is when you realize that they aren't and it doesn't matter.

🐦 Loyalty is rare. If you find it, keep it.

🐦 At the end of the day, you can focus on what is tearing you apart, or what is holding you together.

🐦 At some point you have got to stop crossing oceans for people who wouldn't jump puddles for you.

🕊 When love is not madness, it is not love.

🕊 Being in love with someone is the greatest feeling in the universe.

🐦 A good relationship is with someone who knows all your insecurities and imperfections but still loves you for who you are.

🐦 Life is too short to waste one single second with someone who doesn't appreciate and value you.

🐦 Your actions show where your heart is.

🐦 Three rules in Relationships: don't lie, don't cheat and don't make promises you can't keep.

🕊 Being faithful is easy if you truly love someone.

🕊 Trust and loyalty are a must in any relationship.

🐦 Breakups aren't always meant to make up, sometimes they happen to give you a chance to wake up.

🐦 A great relationship is about two things: First, appreciating the similarities, and second, respecting the differences.

🐦 Appreciate those who love you. Help those who need you. Forgive those who hurt you. Forget those who leave you.

🐦 A true relationship is two imperfect people who refuse to give up on each other.

🐦 Love does great things without expecting great attention; bright lights don't need spot lights.

🐦 If someone doesn't appreciate your presence make him or her appreciate your absence.

🐦 If you are not ready to compromise your wants, you are not ready for a relationship. no relationship will have all your wants.

🐦 The problem is not your mate. Even if you were with someone else and behaved as you do now, it would still be the same situation.

🐦 The best thing in life is to find someone who knows all your flaws, mistakes, and weakness, and still thinks you are completely amazing.

🐦 Do not waste your time on someone who only wants you around when it fits his or her needs.

🐦 Be who you say you are or change what you say. Actions always speak louder than words and your inconsistency will prove you untrustworthy.

🐦 Be with someone who knows your worth.

🕊 Love is not how you listen, but how you understand.

🕊 A true relationship is having someone who accepts your past, supports your present, loves you and encourages your future.

🐦 Sometimes you just outgrow people.

🐦 Love requires sacrifice.

🐦 When your life aligns with love, your
emotions will eventually affirm what
your actions display.

🐦 Don't talk, just act. Don't say, just show.
Don't promise; just prove.

🐦 You cannot master your relationship craft until you've mastered your self.

🐦 You don't give up on someone you love.

🐦 Sometimes it's the ones with the hardest shells that have the softest hearts. Never take advantage of trust.

🐦 The best relationships have a foundation of friendship.

🕊 If there is anything better than to be loved, it is to give love in return.

🕊 If we love people even when they are unlovable, then we provide an opportunity for them to change.

🐦 Apologizing doesn't always mean you're wrong and the other person is right. It means you value your relationship more than your ego.

🐦 Love is not what you feel. Love is what you do. Works, not words, are proof of your love.

🕊 Love can't hide. Love can't be contained. If love is there, you'll know it.

🕊 One of the most amazing traits you can have is forgiveness.

🐦 Putting up walls in relationships don't work. You build them out of pain to keep people out but it actually keeps you trapped in.

🐦 Nothing that is worthwhile is ever easy. Remember that.

🐦 Before you talk, listen. Before you react, think. Before you criticize, wait.

🐦 Always be there for people who matter to you.

🐦 Every time you are able to find some humor in a difficult situation, you win.

🐦 If you can't think of a reason to continue, it's time to start over.

🕊 True love sees your faults and still loves, accepts, and forgives you.

🕊 True love means: I will stand by you, support you, and love you no matter what distance lies between us.

🐦 Relationships fail because we spend too much time pointing out each other's mistakes and not enough time enjoying each other.

🐦 Don't waste your time trying to get people to love you. Spend your time with those who already do.

🕊 Never stay with anyone who puts
you down. Everything they don't like,
someone else will love.

🕊 Be with someone who knows what they
have when they have you.

🐦 Sometimes it takes being away from someone for a while to realize how much you really need him or her in your life.

🐦 If your mate doesn't appreciate you they don't deserve you.

🐦 Relationships are less about finding the right person and more about becoming the right person.

🐦 Find someone who knows how lucky they are to have you.

🐦 You deserve to be with someone who can make you happy, not someone who will complicate your life.

🐦 Bad habits are like a comfortable bed, easy to get into, but hard to get out of.

🕊 Be mindful of what you toss away, be careful of what you push away and think hard before you walk away.

Forgive someone because you believe they are truly sorry, not just because you want to keep them in your life.

🐦 Sometimes you can hurt yourself more than anyone can hurt you just by keeping all your feelings hidden.

🐦 The only way through the pain and hurt is love.

🐦 It's hard to pretend to love someone when you don't, but its harder to pretend not to love someone when you really do.

🐦 Don't let your pride get in the way of what your heart is trying to say.

🐦 Love never left; only our awareness of it diminished.

🐦 Love is always the final and most complete cure to our inner demons.

🐦 True love stands by each other side on good days and stands even closer on bad days.

🐦 Take it day by day. Results don't come overnight. Change doesn't happen immediately.

🕊 Sometimes you have to accept the fact that things will never be how they used to be.

🕊 Every relationship has its problems, but what makes it perfect is if you still want to be together when things go wrong.

🕊 The next time you feel the urge to say I love you, go ahead and say it, it feels great.

🕊 Love exists in all of us and asks for nothing in return. It simply wants someone to open the door.

🐦 Love needs acceptance and gratitude.

🐦 Everybody wants someone to make him or her feel safe in their arms, hold them tight, and remind them everyday that they matter.

🐦 You will never truly understand something until it actually happens to you.

🐦 Sometimes you never know the true value of a moment until it becomes a memory that you wish you could experience again.

🐦 You must fight for the type of relationship you want.

🐦 Always tell someone how you feel, because opportunities are lost in the blink of an eye but regret can last for a lifetime.

🕊 Respect the people who find time in their schedule to see you, and love the people who never look at their schedule when you need them.

🕊 We can't change what we won't confront. Truth is temporarily painful but permanently liberating.

🕊 Never take your mate for granted.

🕊 If someone really loves you, they wouldn't let you slip away.

🕊 Don't walk away because you're scared
to face the situation, walk away when
you've done all you can do to save it.

🕊 Never chase love, affection or attention,
if it isn't given freely by another person,
it isn't worth having.

🐦 You don't have to say I love you to say I love you.

🐦 Love is action not words, people treat you the way they feel about you, words lie but actions do not.

🕊 A real apology is hearing the sadness in their voice, seeing the look in their eyes and realizing they've hurt themselves just as much.

🕊 An apology has three parts, "I'm sorry", "It's my fault", and "How can I make things better", the last part's most important.

🐦 Pain changes people.

🐦 Never put yourself in a situation where you're not sure of where you stand in a person's life.

🐦 Sometimes it's only after you leave a situation that you realize you shouldn't have been in it to begin with.

🐦 When love is true, it isn't broken by problems, or weakened by time.

🐦 Love strives to survive no matter what the circumstances.

🐦 A loving heart is the truest wisdom.

🕊 If a man can't stand by his word don't stand by the man..

🕊 Be careful where you find peace when there's war at home.

🐦 Be with someone who supports, celebrates and inspires you more than anyone else.

🐦 Nothing moves at a faster speed than the beating heart of love.

🐦 The greatest thing you'll ever learn is just to love and be loved in return.

🐦 A person who truly loves you will never let you go, no matter how hard the situation is.

🐦 Breaking a woman's heart is deeper than we realize. It destroys her outlook on love, her future relationships, and her peace within herself.

🐦 The best feeling in the world comes from knowing your presence and absence both mean something to someone.

🐦 Forgiveness does not change the past, but it does enlarge the future.

🐦 Loyalty to others starts with being true to one's self.

🕊 A true relationship is when you can tell each other anything and everything. No secrets and no lies.

🕊 Seven keys to great relationships:
1. Love
2. Respect
3. Vulnerability
4. Communication
5. Forgiveness
6. Loyalty
7. Trust

🕊 Life ends when you stop dreaming, hope ends when you stop believing and love ends when you stop caring.

🕊 Educating the mind without educating the heart is no education at all.

🐦 It takes years to build up trust and only seconds to destroy it.

🐦 Don't underestimate the power of honesty.

🐦 Keep in mind one lie can ruin a thousand truths.

🐦 A supportive woman is worth more than her weight in gold.

🐦 A true relationship is when you can tell each other anything and everything. No secrets and no lies.

🐦 If you judge people, you have no time to love them.

🐦 A relationship isn't a "status", it's a continual commitment to choose another's higher good over your own - even when things get tough.

🐦 People can't see what's in your heart they can only see what you do.

🕊 Take away love and our earth is a tomb.

🕊 The only way to have a friend is to be one.

🐦 Don't forget to share your feelings and say I Love you for you never know what tomorrow will bring.

🐦 The greatest pleasure of life is love.

🐦 When love is real, it doesn't lie, cheat, pretend, or hurt you. It cures you of all your worries and makes you truly happy.

🐦 Age is just a number, maturity is a choice.

🐦 Where there is love there is life.

🐦 Be all in or get all out. There is no halfway.

People fall in love with your heart – not your flaws. You are worthy of love. Your mistakes and imperfections don't define your value.

Stop running away from the problems in your relationship and face them.

🐦 You don't need anybody that doesn't need you.

🐦 Focus on those who truly appreciate you and get rid of those who don't.

🐦 Silence is golden when you can`t think of a good answer.

🐦 Sometimes the words we leave unspoken are the most important ones that should have been said.

🕊 Cuddle with your mate, look into his or her eyes and say, "I love you."

🕊 Be selective in your battles. Sometimes peace is better than being right.

🐦 Mistakes are always forgivable, if one has the courage to admit them.

🐦 The hardest decision is to figure out if you want to walk away or try harder.

PART FOUR

MAKE EVERY DAY SPECIAL

"We accept the love we think we deserve."

- Stephen Chbosky

🐦 Love is a continual choice to put others' needs above your own - even when it's inconvenient, undesirable or difficult.

🐦 Love does not equal to complicity.

🕊 Love is a language spoken by everyone but understood only by the heart.

🕊 It is important to stop and enjoy the person you are with.

🐦 Sometimes music is all you need.

🐦 Life has no rewind, but it is being recorded.

🕊 You don't really need someone to complete you. You only need someone to accept you completely.

🕊 Kiss your mate in a way that will stay with him or her until they see you again.

🐦 There is no happy relationship, just two happy people in a relationship.

🐦 Every day is a gift. Unwrap it slowly.

🐦 Slow down and enjoy the journey, right now.

🐦 Don't wait for the perfect moment.. Take the moment and make it perfect.

🐦 Take time for the people in your life. They won't always be there.

🐦 You can't expect to get great results from mediocre effort. You get out what you put in.

🐦 Love doesn't have to be complicated, it's just has to be intentional. Hold a door, share a smile, or lend a listening ear.

🐦 There is power in little gifts of love.

🐦 Nothing in a relationship should be forced. You should want to be faithful. You should want to see them happy. If not, you should leave.

🐦 The only difference between a good day and a bad day is your attitude.

🐦 If you have the power to make someone happy, do it.

🐦 Be the reason someone smiles today.

🐦 If your mate is important to you, show them.

🐦 Every woman deserves a man who respects her, and every man deserves a woman who appreciates his effort.

🐦 Yesterday is far away and tomorrow is a long way off. So, make the best of today.

🐦 Never miss an opportunity to tell someone how much he or she means to you.

🐦 We tend to forget that happiness doesn't come as a result of getting something we don't have, but of appreciating what we do have.

🐦 If you want successful relationships, you need to put some structure around them because they do not happen by accident.

🐦 The goal is to help people become everything they really are. Not what you want them to be.

🐦 Don't judge until you know all the facts and once you know don't judge.

🐦 The little things mean the most.

🐦 It's nice when someone remembers small details about you.

🕊 Never abuse the forgiving spirit of a woman.

🕊 Commit to making your mate happy today by giving them attention, appreciation, and affection.

🐦 The best feeling in the world is being loved back by the person you love.

🐦 Anything you truly want must be worth fighting for.

🐦 If you want to share someone's heart,
share their values, support their dreams
and be a source of peace and enjoyment.

🐦 Everyone wants to know they are
valuable. Tell your mate today that they
matter.

🕊 Slow down and enjoy the journey and take time for the people in your life.

🕊 Time has a way of showing us what really matters.

🐦 Appreciate the little things that you like about your mate.

🐦 Good relationships don't just happen. They take time, patience, and two people who truly want to be together.

🐦 The best things happen unexpectedly.

Anyone that encourages intellectual, emotional, artistic or spiritual growth is a keeper.

🐦 Always know the difference between what you're getting and what you deserve.

🐦 It's not about "having" time. It's about making time.

🐦 If you allow someone to be who he or she is and they allow you to be who you are, then that's love. Anything else is torture.

🐦 Laugh when you can, apologize when you should, and let go of what you can't change.

🐦 It's better to treat someone right before someone else comes along to do the job for you.

🐦 Sometimes, change is what we need.

🐦 Sometimes we don't appreciate what we already have because we're too focused on what we want.

🐦 Everything gets better with time.

🐦 Appreciate the relationship you have with your mate, because the future can take it all away from you anytime.

🐦 Don't get so caught up in what could be and start appreciating what is.

🐦 Life is too short to spend it with people who don't make you happy.

🐦 The sooner you realize it's never going to go back to the way it was, the sooner you will move on.

🕊 Stop wishing for something to happen and go make it happen.

🕊 Love is a basic human emotion, but understanding how and why it happens is not necessarily easy.

🐦 It's never too late to start appreciating your mate.

🐦 You can only try your best. And if they can't appreciate that, it's their fault, not yours.

🐦 Nobody cares if you can`t dance well.
Just get up and dance.

🐦 Words mean nothing until they're
proven and shown.

🐦 Joy is the experience of being loved.

🐦 Always smile more than you cry, give
   more than what you take, and love more
   than you hate.

🐦 Three things you cannot recover in life: the word after its said, the moment after its missed, and the time after its gone.

🐦 A person needs just three things to be truly happy in the world: someone to love, something to do, and something to hope for.

🐦 Never give up. Great things take time.

"Love wholeheartedly, be surprised,
give thanks and praise- then you will
discover the fullness of your life."
- Brother David Steindl-Rast

"You know you're in love when you can't fall asleep because reality is finally better than your dreams."

– Dr. Seuss.

"Love is that condition in which the happiness of another person is essential to your own."

– Robert A. Heinlein

"The best love is the kind that awakens the soul; that makes us reach for more, that plants that fire in our hearts and brings peace to our minds. That's what I hope to give you forever."

- The Notebook

AFTER THOUGHTS FROM THE AUTHOR

It's never too late to be what you could have been. Start today adjusting your attitude and outlook, and your results for ensuring a productive lifestyle will be made more effectively. Wherever you are in your life, let *THE HOPE HANDBOOK* guide you in a new direction to a new start, in helping you realize how much control you have over your own life.

Always remember, we create the hope or the fear in our lives by the thoughts and ideas we put into action.

ABOUT THE AUTHOR

With more than a decade of experience, **Germany Kent**, also known as The Hope Guru™, has enjoyed a successful consulting business with clients from all walks of life. Germany is a dynamic public speaker. She has been awarded multiple times for speaking.

She has appeared nationally on The Drs, The Food Network, NBC, CBS, ABC, Disney, MTV, and BET, just to name a few.

She was previously listed in Who's Who Among Young Americans.

As Germany's brand has grown, both domestic and internationally, she has picked up more than a few fans who remain interested in her status. This has catapulted her into a category of respected power and influence, especially on social media, where she has been cited as a top social media influencer.

Germany is dedicated and committed to giving back to the community. She is dedicated to helping others reach their highest potential. She engages herself as a coach and mentor, another platform that Germany is immensely committed too.

Germany graduated with honors from The University of Alabama and Mississippi State University. She resides in Southern California where she is an entertainment host and successful commercial actress. As a media personality, Germany has interviewed power players, newsmakers and Hollywood royalty. She has landed interviews with Oscar, Emmy, Golden Globe, and Grammy-award winning performers.

Germany offers messages of HOPE on Twitter and continues to be a social media magnet.

You can follow her @germanykent to receive her messages of motivation and inspiration onto your timeline.

TO OUR READERS

Star Stone Press, publishes books on topics ranging from spirituality, personal growth and self-help to inspiration, technology, family, and social titles. Our mission is to publish quality books that will contribute to the wellbeing of the reader.

Our readers are our most important resource, and we value your input and ideas. Please feel free to contact us.

Mail to:

Star Stone Press
10736 Jefferson Blvd #164
Culver City, CA 90230

Message From Germany
If you have enjoyed my book, please consider writing and posting a customer review at Amazon.com, Goodreads.com and/or LibraryThing.com. I would really appreciate your support.

Visit Germany on the web at:
www.TheHopeGuru.com